ME AND MY GRANDDADDY

MY GRANDDADDY AND ME

Written by Ricquell Goolsby

Pictures by Rahul Roy

Me and My Granddaddy, My Granddaddy and Me

iUniverse books may be ordered through booksellers or by contacting:

iUniverse
1663 Liberty Drive
Bloomington, IN 47403
www.iuniverse.com
844-349-9409

ISBN: 978-1-6632-1608-3 (sc)
ISBN: 978-1-6632-1609-0 (e)

Library of Congress Control Number: 2021900498

Print information available on the last page.

iUniverse rev. date: 03/04/2021

This book is dedicated to the life and legacy of Preston V. Batten Sr. The perfect blend of humility, confidence, strength, intelligence, perseverance, and love. His laugh would fill a room. His smile brightened my life.   His love and memories inspired this book. I love you granddaddy…… *"I love you too granddaughter"*

I love my granddaddy and he loves me

I like to help him work on his truck under the big tree

My granddaddy is strong, there is
nothing that he can't do

When he drinks his morning coffee, I drink a cup too

We love to sing while he drives me to school

We share a special bond that's oh so cool

We watch funny shows and granddaddy laughs "tee heehe"

He teaches me to work hard and believes in me

He is really the best and that's no lie
My granddaddy is my favorite guy

He is kind and caring, gentle and sweet
When we dance he even lets me stand on his feet

At the end of the day when it's time for bed
Into my room he peaks his head

I love you granddaughter......
I love you too granddaddy

Printed in the United States
by Baker & Taylor Publisher Services